Becoming VICE PRESIDENT

By Maria Nelson

Gareth Stevens
PUBLISHING

Please visit our website, www.garethstevens.com. For a free color catalog of all our high-quality books, call toll free 1-800-542-2595 or fax 1-877-542-2596.

Library of Congress Cataloging-in-Publication Data

Nelson, Maria.
  Becoming vice president / Maria Nelson.
      pages cm. — (Who's your candidate? Choosing government leaders)
  Includes index.
  ISBN 978-1-4824-4055-3 (pbk.)
  ISBN 978-1-4824-4056-0 (6 pack)
  ISBN 978-1-4824-4057-7 (library binding)
  1. Vice-Presidents—United States—Juvenile literature. I. Title.
  JK609.5.N44 2016
  352.23'90973—dc23

                                        2015031505

Published in 2016 by
Gareth Stevens Publishing
111 East 14th Street, Suite 349
New York, NY 10003

Copyright © 2016 Gareth Stevens Publishing

Designer: Andrea Davison-Bartolotta
Editor: Kristen Nelson

Photo credits: Cover, p. 1 (boy) ranplett/Getty Images; cover, p. 1 (white house) Avatarmin/Getty Images; pp. 4, 14, 15, 22, 23 courtesy of the Library of Congress; p. 5 Dirk Anschutz/Getty Images; p. 7 Marshall/Liaison/Getty Images; p. 8 Ariel Skelley/Getty Images; pp. 8–9 PhotoQuest/Getty Images; p. 10 Karl Schumacher/The LIFE Images Collection/Getty Images; p. 11 Chip Somodevilla/Getty Images; p. 13 GraphicaArtis/Getty Images; p. 16 Independent Picture Service/Getty Images; p. 17 Popperfoto/Getty Images; p. 19 National Archives/Newsmakers/ Getty Images; p. 20 Thomas Trutschel/Photothek via Getty Images; p. 21 Mandel Ngan/Getty Images; p. 25 David Hume Kennerly/Getty Images; pp. 26–27 Cultura RM/Nancy Honey/Getty Images; p. 28 jiawangkun/ Shutterstock.com; p. 29 Image Source/Getty Images.

Printed in the United States of America

CPSIA compliance information: Batch #CW16GS: For further information contact Gareth Stevens, New York, New York at 1-800-542-2595.

CONTENTS

Words in the glossary appear in **bold** type the first time they are used in the text.

Call for Change

No matter how old you are, you can make a difference in the world around you. Much of the year, you spend most of your time in school. Are there things you'd change about the activities your school offers? Do you have a good idea for a student-led **tutoring** group? If your school has student leadership organizations such as a student council, you might be able to speak up and work to make those changes!

Similarly, the vice president of the United States can have a real effect on what happens in the US government—and therefore the country!

It Depends

The level of **involvement** of the vice president in the running of the US government depends on the person in the position and what the president wants him or her to do. Some have a calendar packed with meetings and an **agenda**. But others are more laid-back. Henry Wilson, the second vice president of Ulysses S. Grant, wrote a book while in office!

Grant   Wilson

Sometimes student elections are based on popularity. While it's nice to have people simply like you, having leadership skills and goals for your school make you a better student leader!

According to the US **Constitution**, the vice president only has a few jobs. First, the vice president takes the place of the president if he or she can't serve.

Second, the vice president is the president of the Senate, which is one of the two **legislative** bodies that make up the US Congress. The Senate is made up of 100 state representatives, two from each state. Because there's an even number of senators, a tie is possible when they vote. The vice president doesn't have a vote in the Senate unless that happens. Then he or she can be the tiebreaker!

Legislative vs. Executive

When John Adams was vice president, he cast 29 tie-breaking votes, the most of any vice president. Modern vice presidents don't spend a lot of time in the Senate, unless their vote is needed. They've become more a part of the executive branch of government, which is headed by the president.

According to the Constitution, the vice president is also the person who announces the winner of the presidential election to both houses of Congress: the Senate and the House of Representatives.

Al Gore

Who Qualifies?

Since the vice president could become the president someday, he or she must meet certain requirements in order to be elected. The vice president must be:

- 35 years of age or older.

- a natural-born US citizen (born in the United States or to parents who are US citizens).

- a resident of the United States for at least 14 years.

Your Turn!

Some school leadership positions require that you collect a certain number of signatures on a **petition** before you can run. This can take a lot of time, so don't wait until the last minute! Attend sports games and other school activities to find enough people to sign. Be sure to ask nicely!

The road to becoming vice president is often a long one for politicians. In general, vice presidents have been older men, many of whom are in their 50s and 60s. That makes sense considering the average age of the US president when elected is about 55 years old.

Harry Truman

Alben Barkley

Alben Barkley was the oldest vice president when he was elected at age 72.

Former vice president Dan Quayle once said the major responsibility of the vice president is "to be prepared." Knowledge of the inner workings of the US government is of utmost importance for a vice president. Most vice presidents have a lot of political experience to draw from by the time they reach the position.

Vice Presidents Spiro Agnew and Nelson Rockefeller were state governors before they were vice president. George H. W. Bush, who served as a vice president for 8 years before being elected president, had been in the House of Representatives and worked for the Central Intelligence Agency.

Your Turn!

Experience is often important for students running for higher leadership positions. If you'd like to be the vice president of a school organization someday, start with something smaller such as heading the school dance committee. You could also be a team captain or the stage manager for a play. Many activities can build and show off your leadership skills!

President Ronald Regan

Vice President George H. W. Bush

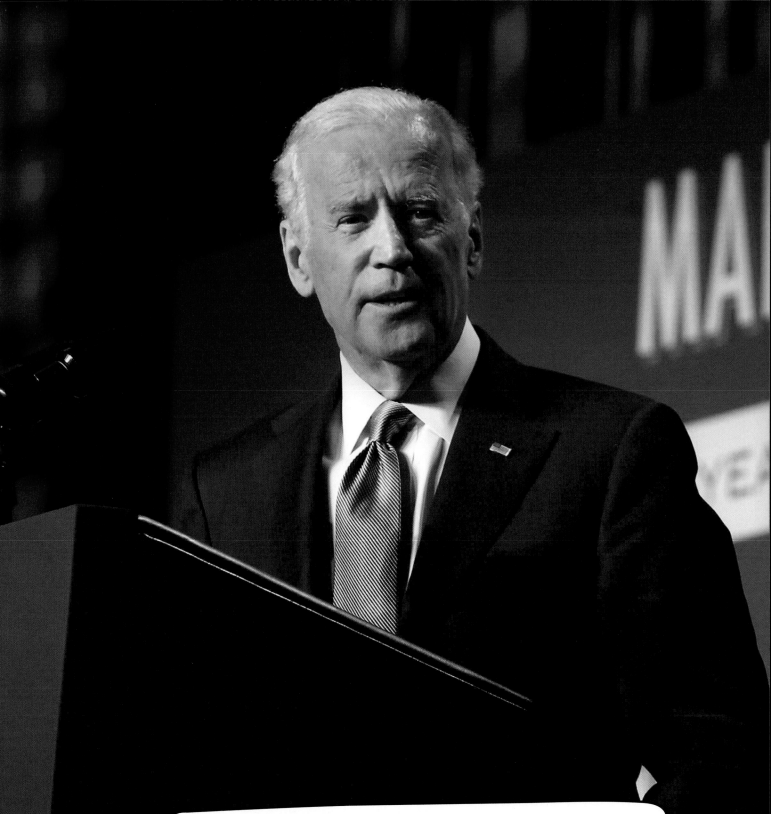

Before becoming vice president, Joe Biden served for 36 years in the Senate, representing Delaware.

The Electoral College

The first vice presidents of the United States were actually running for president! The US Constitution set up a process for electing president and vice president called the Electoral College.

Here's how it worked: A group of electors was chosen within each state, one for each senator and House representative the state had in Congress. Each would cast two votes for president, one of which had to be for a candidate not from their state. The person who received the majority of votes became president. The person with the second-greatest number of votes became vice president. That's how John Adams and Thomas Jefferson became vice president!

Your Turn!

Your school's student council positions may be decided in the same way early US vice presidents were chosen. If you run for student council president and receive the second-greatest number of votes and become vice president, that's okay! All leadership experiences can help you achieve your future goals.

During the early years of the United States, state loyalty was more important to most people than national loyalty. That's why electors had to vote for someone not from their state, too.

This system was only in place for a few presidential elections. During the election of 1800, Thomas Jefferson and Aaron Burr both received the same number of electoral votes. According to the Constitution, that sent the presidential election to the House of Representatives. However, the House voted 35 times without a winner! Finally, Jefferson was chosen as president, making Burr vice president. It was clear the Electoral College as it was didn't work well.

Jefferson

When Thomas Jefferson became John Adams's vice president, he was thought to be a great political mind in his own right. However, he had different ideas than Adams about how the country should be run. So, during his vice presidency, he prepared himself to run for president in 1800 and wrote a book about how the vice president should lead the Senate.

By the next presidential election, Congress had passed the Twelfth **Amendment**. Now, the Electoral College voted for the offices of president and vice president separately. That's how it's done today!

EIGHTH CONGRESS OF THE UNITED STATES;

AT THE FIRST SESSION,

Begun and held at the city of Washington, in the territory of Columbia, on Monday, the seventeenth of October, one thousand eight hundred and three.

Resolved by the Senate and House of Representatives of the United States of America, in Congress assembled,

Twelfth Amendment to the Constitution

The rise of political parties is one of the reasons the original design of the Electoral College didn't work. Aaron Burr, shown here, and Thomas Jefferson were both part of the Democratic-Republican Party.

Running Mates

Candidates for US president and vice president usually run for office together, or "share the ticket." Despite being voted for separately by the Electoral College, these pairs, or running mates, have always been elected together.

Leaders of the political party a presidential candidate represents often choose the candidate's running mate. A vice presidential candidate may be chosen because he or she is a respected member of the party. Or the presidential candidate may need support from a part of the country in which the vice presidential candidate is popular. Vice presidential candidates may have an effect on the outcome of an election, so choosing the right one is important!

Your Turn!

Are you someone's running mate? School elections may have students run on a ticket with someone else, too. Agreeing to be someone's vice president, should they win, is a big deal. Make sure you know what the campaign and the job will include before you say yes.

presidential campaign pin

CLINTON ☆ GORE
NEW LEADERSHIP IN '92

Running mates aren't necessarily friends, and in fact, may not even know each other before running together. President Richard Nixon may have never met Spiro Agnew before Agnew became his running mate!

Richard Nixon

Spiro Agnew

Once chosen as a running mate, a vice presidential candidate has to hit the campaign trail! Like the presidential candidates, candidates for vice president have to take part in **debates** and travel around the country meeting voters. They often have a main message they're trying to make sure people know. This is often the same message as their running mate, and they need to know it as well as the presidential candidate.

Vice presidential candidates may campaign for more than a year. But once the sitting vice president announces a win, the incoming vice president gets even busier!

Running Alone?

Vice presidential candidates *can* run for office without a presidential candidate. In 1972, Endicott Peabody used the **slogan** "The number one man for the number two job" in his candidacy for vice president. More commonly, candidates run a campaign within their own party, trying to be chosen for a spot on the big ticket.

A Modern Role

The first US vice president, John Adams, said the job was "the most insignificant office that ever the invention of man **contrived**." The vice president's **role** has changed and grown a lot since he held the office!

Today, those who become vice president are given responsibilities by the president. This often includes meeting with leaders of other countries and speaking to Congress about the president's agenda. The vice president is often a close advisor to the president and may attend **cabinet** meetings. He or she supports the president in many ways, including representing the president at events around the world.

Your Turn!

When in a supportive leadership position such as vice president, your opinion can be very important. Taking the time to listen to all sides of an issue and considering each fairly can help you give the president good advice. Always be honest about what you think and why. This can help your organization make the best decision possible.

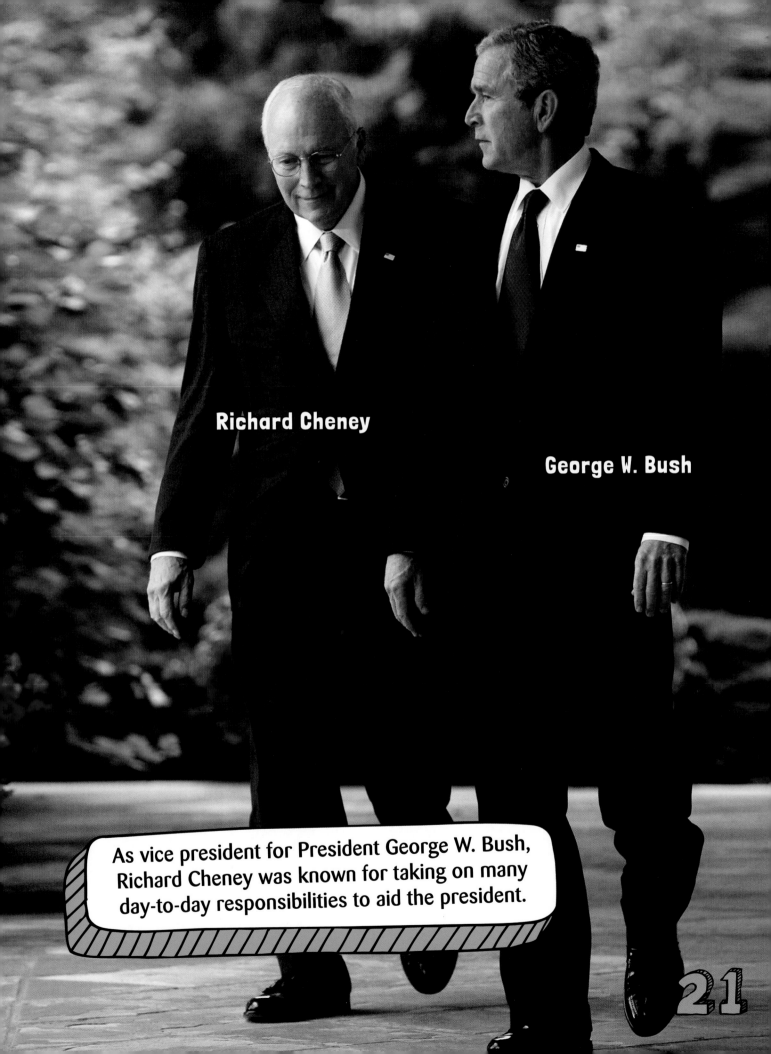

Richard Cheney

George W. Bush

As vice president for President George W. Bush, Richard Cheney was known for taking on many day-to-day responsibilities to aid the president.

Clarifying the Constitution

The vice president has many duties. But nothing on his or her calendar is more important than the main role of the vice president—to succeed the president if needed.

The Constitution says the power of the president will "devolve on," or move to, the vice president. No one needed to question what this meant until 1841 when President William Henry Harrison died. Vice President John Tyler made a big move. He decided the Constitution's words meant that since the "powers and duties" of the president devolved on the vice president, the whole of the office did!

Teddy Roosevelt

Theodore Roosevelt was already a well-known political figure when he became the vice president under President William McKinley, who was beginning his second term in 1901. When McKinley was killed 6 months after the election, Roosevelt succeeded him. In 1904, Roosevelt became the first vice president to win his own presidential election following a succession.

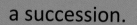

President John Tyler set a precedent by taking the office of president after President Harrison died. A precedent is something done or said that's used as an example for future people in the role. The Twenty-Fifth Amendment made his precedent law.

Becoming...President!

The vice president needs to be prepared to become president, but it doesn't happen that often. Only 14 vice presidents have succeeded to the presidency. Eight of those 14 took office because a president died. One succeeded a president who resigned, or left office. Four were elected president in their own right after serving as vice president, and one became president years after serving as vice president. In general though, becoming US vice president isn't considered a sure path to the presidency.

Some vice presidents have served as "acting president" for a time. In 1985, 2002, and 2007, presidents had medical **procedures**, and their vice presidents took over until they were well.

Succeeding the VP

What if both the president and vice president die or resign? Then the country looks to the Presidential Succession Law of 1947, which states the Speaker of the House would be next in line for the presidency, followed by the president pro tempore of the Senate. Both these positions are chosen by the majority party and are often leaders in that party.

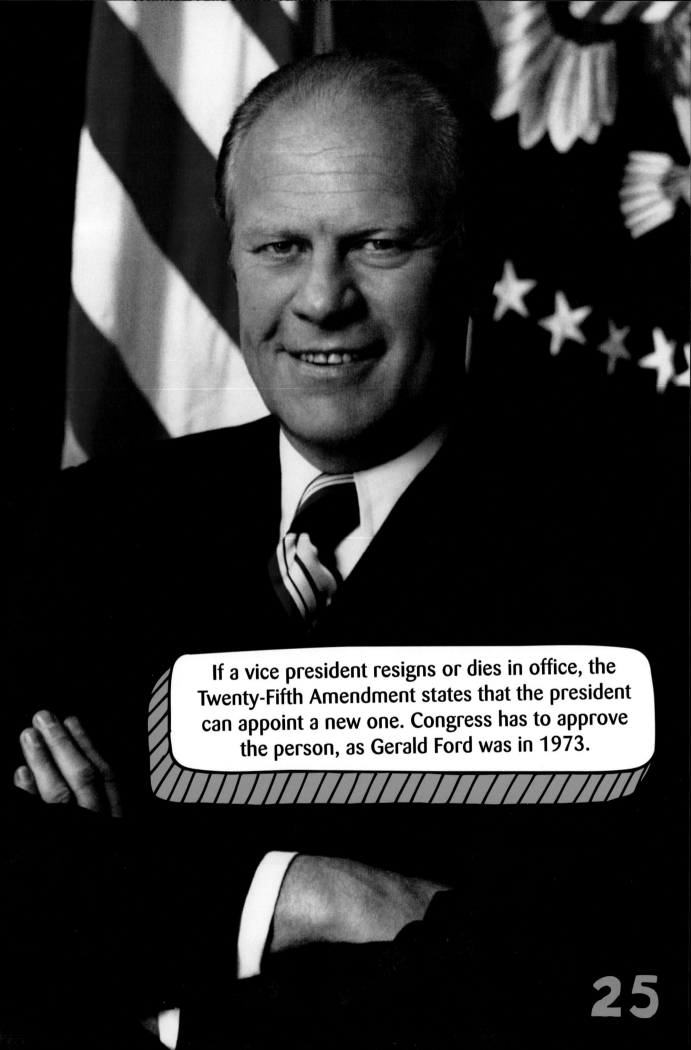

If a vice president resigns or dies in office, the Twenty-Fifth Amendment states that the president can appoint a new one. Congress has to approve the person, as Gerald Ford was in 1973.

Your Stepping-Stone!

Are you running for student council vice president because you'd like to be the president of a student organization someday? That's a good move! By campaigning for vice president or another lower leadership position, you'll gain valuable experience you can use as president. You'll also make other students and teachers at your school familiar with your name and abilities. This can help you earn more votes next time you're campaigning!

Your Turn!

Not everyone wants to be president. The vice president of a student organization can certainly be a role that works more behind the scenes, and that might make it a good fit for you. Let others know that your skills as a speechwriter or organizer are great qualities, especially paired with others who are outgoing.

If you're using a student leadership position as a stepping-stone to something greater, make the most of it. Set a few small goals to accomplish—and remember to take credit for your hard work!

You don't have to be outspoken to be a leader. Anyone who wants to make a difference and can come up with a clear plan on how to do so can be an effective leader!

Student leadership positions like vice president of student council can lead to a career in politics someday—perhaps even the federal vice presidency! What can you do to reach your goals?

- Pay attention in school, especially when learning how the US government works.

- Go to college. Modern vice presidents often go on to get a master's degree or study law, too.

- Practice public speaking. Learn how to get your message across in short, clear statements.

- Travel. Vice presidents need to know how to talk to many different kinds of people!

- Hold leadership positions in your school and community.

- Start working on local political campaigns.

Members of the House of Representatives only have to be 25 to be elected. You can start your political career soon after finishing college if you want!

GLOSSARY

agenda: things someone wants to get done or talk about

amendment: a change or addition to a constitution

cabinet: a group of senior officials appointed by the president as special advisors

constitution: the basic laws by which a country or state is governed

contrive: to form or think of

debate: an argument or public discussion

influential: having an effect on

involvement: the state of being a part of something

legislative: having to do with making laws

petition: a written request signed by many people

procedure: an operation or other medical treatment

role: the part someone has in a group

slogan: a word or phrase that's easy to remember and grabs attention

tutoring: having to do with helping students individually with schoolwork

BOOKS

Bow, James. *What Is the Executive Branch?* New York, NY: Crabtree Publishing Company, 2013.

Gunderson, Megan M. *Andrew Johnson.* Edina, MN: ABDO, 2009.

Landau, Elaine. *The President, Vice President, and Cabinet: A Look at the Executive Branch.* Minneapolis, MN: Lerner Publications, 2012.

WEBSITES

Three Branches of Government
kids.usa.gov/three-branches-of-government/index.shtml
Review the branches of the US government.

U.S. Senate: Vice President of the United States
www.senate.gov/artandhistory/history/common/briefing/Vice_President.htm
Find out more about the history of the vice presidential office.

INDEX